PHP INTERVIEW QUESTIONS AND ANSWERS

TOWARDS PROGRAMMING KNOWLEDGE

AVINASH NANASAHEB PAGAR

I would like to dedicate this book to my students.

Avinash Nanasaheb Pagar

Contents

CHAPTER ONE

PHP Interview Questions and Answers

1. What is PHP?

a. PHP is popular **Server side** scripting language.

b. It is used for fast **web development** bycreating **dynamic web pages.**

c. PHP stands for **Hypertext Preprocessor.**

d. It is **open source** and free to use and **easy** to learn.

2. Who invent PHP Language?

Sir **Rasmus Lerdorf** invent PHP and known as father of PHP.

3. What is the current version of PHP?

As January 2022 **PHP version is 7.4.**

4. What is the use of 'echo' in PHP?

a. Echo is statement, used to print data in web page or display output.

b.It is language construct, not a function.

c. It doesn't return any value.

d. It is used without and with parenthesis. echo or echo();

5. What is the difference between echo and print ()?

echo and print statements both are used as a language construct. There is some differences between them are

1. echo statement doesn't return any value. While print return always value integer type.

2. echo statement is faster than print statement.

3. In echo statement multiple values are passed and separated by, comma.

4. In print statement can't pass multiple parameters.

5. echo statement used without and with parenthesis. echo or echo();

6. What is the use of print_r () function?

Print_r() function is used to print the output in human readable format.

7. How to include file in PHP page?

In PHP file can be included using two function by **include () or by require ()**, by passing parameter as a file path.

8. Differentiate between include () and require ()?

Include() and require() both are used to include specific file in web page.

By using **include()** if file is not found, a warning will be issued. And execution of script will continue.

By using **require()** if file is not found, a fatal error will occur and execution of script will halt.

9. What is the difference between require () and require_once ()?

Both require and require_once functions performed same task to include file in script. Only difference between them is require_once check before executing the script, that script is already included or not.

10. List different types of variables in PHP?

Total eight different data type in PHP-

a. NULL
b. Booleans
c. Integers
d. Doubles
e. Strings
f. Arrays
g. Resources
h. Objects

11.How can we get the IP Address of the client?

$_SERVER ["REMOTE_ADDR"]; variable gives the IP Address of the client.

12. Differentiate between GET and POST?

Main Difference between Get and POST are

1. Generally POST method used in data handling operations like insert data and update data in database, while Get method is used to retrieve data.
2. By using Get we can send maximum 2048 characters of data. While using POST method there is no restrictions of data.
3. Get can handles ASCII type of data. POST can handles binary type of data.
4. Get is less secure. POST is secure method to transfer data.
5. In Get request data is shown in the URL. While data is not shown in the POST request in URL, It is encoded form.

13. **What is the difference between PHP4 and PHP5?**

PHP4 doesn't support OOPS while PHP5 supports **Object Oriented Programming Features**.

14. What is session? Why we use it?

Session is a technique to store or preserve information across web pages, to retrieve information for further use. In PHP session variables are used with the global variable **$_SESSION.** HTTP means **Hypertext Transfer Protocol** which is stateless. It can't be able to handle data or information in subsequent pages, so to access data in multiple pages session is used.

Session started using **session_start()** function. We can track each user on web application by unique session id.

15. Where session is stored?

We can store Session in **database**. Session is available on server in temporary file.

16. What is the default session time?

The default session time in PHP is until the user close the browser. We can use **session_write_close()** function to end session manually.

17. How to get the current session id?

In PHP the current session id can be get using **session_id ()** function.

18. How to get the current session id?

In PHP the current session id can be get using **session_id ()** function.

19. Differentiate session_unset () and session_unregister ().

The **session_unset()** function is used to free all session variables. The **session_unregister**() variable is used to unregister the variables from the session.

20. How can pass variables in subsequent pages in PHP?

We can pass variables in subsequent pages by using cookie, session or hidden fields.

21. What is cookie? Why we use it?

Cookie is simple text type file which is available on client's computer. We can set and retrieve information from cookie. The user information identified using cookie which is stored in client browser.

22. How to set the value in Cookie?

In PHP cookie value is set using function setcookie ("fruit", "mango", time () +3600);

23. How to retrieve value from cookie?

To set value in cookie - setcookie ("fruit", "mango", time () +3600);

To retrieve value from the cookie – echo $COOKIE["user"];

24. What is persistent cookie?

Persistent cookie is the type of cookie which is stored on client's computer browser permanently. Normally, cookies files are stored on the browser of the client's computer temporarily. Users can check the persistent cookies files so persistent cookies are less secure than the temporary cookies.

25. Differentiate between explode () and split () function?

explode() and split() function perform same functionality. Basic function is to split string into array.

26. Differentiate between explode() and implode() functions.

explode() function is used to split or break the given string into array. While implode () function returns a string from the given array.

For example: - explode function

$strVar = "welcome everyone, have a nice day";

print_r (explode (" ", $strVar));

Output: -

[0] => welcome

[1] => everyone
[2] => have
[3] => a
[4] => nice
[5] => day

For example: - implode function

$arrImplode = array ('welcome','to','php','world');
echo implode (" ", $arrImplode);

Output:-

Welcome to php world.

27. Explain error types in PHP?

There are three types of errors in PHP.

a. **Notice** – Notice are categorized in simple and non critical type of errors.
b. **Warning** – Warnings are categorized in more important than notice type errors. Warnings display during script execution. Script executes continuously.
c. **Fatal Errors** – Fatal errors are categorized in critical type errors. A fatal error occurs during the script execution. Fatal errors can terminate the execution of the script.

28. **How we can enable error reporting in PHP?**

We can enable error reporting in PHP using different ways.-

1. To make change in **PHP.ini** file set display_errors on OR
2. In PHP script add or include **Ini_set("display_errors","1")** in your script.

29. Differentiate between unset () and unlink ()?

Unset is used to set the file undefined. Unlink is used to delete the file. Both are related to file system.

30. What is PEAR stand for?

PEAR stands for **PHP Extension Application Repository.** It is designed for special purpose for developers to provide high level of function libraries to accelerate the development speed and maximize production.

31. Is multiple inheritances supported in PHP language?

No, multiple inheritance doesn't support in PHP. PHP only supports **single inheritance.** Single inheritance can handle using 'extended' keyword.

32. What are traits?

Traits are technique or way by which we can create reusable code in PHP type languages where single inheritance is not supported. So traits mechanism is useful in that situation.

33. How can image functionality implemented in PHP?

Image functionality is implemented in PHP using **GD Library.** It provides the image functions.

34. What is the purpose of imagetypes () function?

Imagetypes () function provides the **image format** and **image types** of selected image.

35. Explain Image properties functions?

Different image property functions provide image size, image width and image height.

1. Image size provided by – getimagesize () function.
2. Image width provided by – imagesx () function.
3. Image height provided by – imagesy () function.

36. What is final class and final method?

Final class means the class which is declared as final **can't be extended**. And Final method means the methods **can't be overridded**. It is introduced in PHP 5 version.

37. How can check given variable is empty?

empty() function is used to check given variable is empty or not.

38. How can check the value of given variable is numeric or not?

Is_numeric() function is used to check given variable is numeric or not.

39. How can check the value of given variable is alphanumeric or not?

Ctype_alnum is used to check given variable is alphanumeric or not.

40. In PHP script how can we define constant?

By using define() directive we can define constant.

define("submarks", 99);

41. Can we change the value of constant during script execution?

No, we can't change the value of the constant during PHP script execution.

42. How can check the given variable is set or not?

A Boolean function is used to check whether given variable is set or not.

43. Name the function returns the number of elements in array.

Using count () function we can get the number of elements in array.

44. What is the use of in_array () function.

In_array () function used to check the value is exist in array or not.

45. Write any 6 array functions in PHP.

Some of the array functions in PHP

1. array () – used to create array.
2. array_push () - used to insert one or more elements at the end of array.
3. array_pop () – used to delete the last element from the array.
4. array_reverse () – used to returns array elements in reverse order.
5. array_sum () – used to calculate sum of values of array.
6. In_array () – used to check given values is exists in array.
7. array_product () - used to calculate product of values of array.
8. array_merge () – used to merge one or more array in one array.

46. Explain different types of array sorting methods.
Following are the sorting functions in PHP

1. Sort()
2. Rsort()
3. Asort()
4. Arsort()
5. Ksort()
6. Krsort()

47. Write any 6 string function in PHP.
Following are the string functions in PHP

1. echo – used to outputs one or more string.
2. Strlen () – used to returns the length of the string.

3. Strcmp () – used to compare two string on case sensitive basis.
4. Explode () – used to breaks the string into array.
5. Implode () – used to get a string from the elements of the array.
6. Strtolower () - used to convert string into lowercase.
7. Strtoupper () – used to convert string into uppercase.
8. Strrev () – used to returns a string in reverse order.
9. Str_split () – used to split string into array.

48. How can we get number of parameters passed into a function?

func_num_args () function is used to get the number of parameters passed into a function.

49. How to protect special characters in a query string?

We can protect special characters in a query string by using urlencode() function.

50. How can we submit a form using button?

We can submit a form using document.submit.form() function.

CHAPTER TWO

Codeigniter Interview Questions and Answers

1. What is CodeIgniter?

a. It is Open Source Framework
b. Codeigniter framework is used to develop web application in PHP.
c. Codeigniter framework is easy to use as compared to other framework.
d. It is loosely based MVC pattern framework.
e. It is similar to Cake PHP.
f. CodeIgniter is light weighted.

2. What is the current version of CodeIgniter?

Current version of Codeigniter is 4.0 - Released date September 2019.

3. What is stable version of CodeIgniter?

Stable version of CodeIgniter is 3.1.10 – Released date January 2019.

4. In which language Codeigniter is written?

Codeigniter is written in PHP.

5. What is the way to check or find CodeIgniter version?

Codeigniter version can be check using following steps

a. Go to system/core/Codeigniter.php
b. Check CI_VERSION constant value define('CI_VERSION', '3.0.5');

6. Explain Features of CodeIgniter.

a. Codeigniter is open source framework.
b. It is easy to use as compared to other frameworks in PHP
c. Codeigniter also free to use.
d. Based on MVC based pattern for faster development.
e. CodeIgniter having Query builder.
f. It is very lightweight framework in PHP.
g. Codeigniter having featured database classes for support different platforms.
h. Codeigniter having excellent documentation.
a. Also it is extensible. This feature is done with the help of libraries, helpers and system hooks.
j. Classes and functions for Security, XSS filtering and Error logging.

7. What is the database supported to CodeIgniter?

Database supported to CodeIgniter.

a. MySQL
b. PostgreSQL
c. SQLite
d. Oracle
e. Firebird

f. CUBRID

8. Explain Model-View-Controller in CodeIgniter.

Codeigniter is loosely based on MVC pattern. It is used for separate presentation login from the business logic using MVC.

Model – The Models class contains the data structure of application. They are managed by controller. Model class contains functions to perform various operations like Insert, Update and Delete information in database. It is stored in application/models directory.

Ex.

```
Class Modelname CI_Model
{
Public function__construct
{
Parent::__construct();
}
}
```

View – View having information with interface design displayed on the browser that is being presented to user. Views never directly called. It is called with the help of controller in Codeigniter. It is stored in application/views directory.

Controller - Controller is intermediate between model and view to control process between them. Also contains resources which are required to process HTTP request of application. It is stored in application/controller directory.

9. Explain how to load model in CodeIgniter.

By including following code in controller.

$this->load->model ('Model_Name');

10. Explain how to load view in CodeIgniter.

By including following code in controller.

$this->load->view('View_Name');

11. Explain or Write how to access Config variable in CodeIgniter?

$this->Config->item ('variable_name');

12. How to unset session in CodeIgniter?

Session in Codeigniter unset using code as -

$this->session->unset_userdata('some_name');

13. How to get last insert id in CodeIgniter?

Get last insert id in CodeIgniter.

$this->db->insert_id();

14. What are helpers in Codeigniter?

Helpers are file contains collection of functions in a particular category. Helpers are written in procedural programming. Not written in Object Oriented Format. Every helper performs particular functionality.

15. How to load helper files?

Helper files include using code as -

$this->load->helper ('helper_name');

16. What is the process to load multiple helper files?

In CodeIgniter multiple helper files loaded using code -

$this->load->helper (array ('helperfile1', 'helperfile2', 'helperfile3'));

17. What are different types of helpers?

Different types of helpers are given below.

a. Form Helpers – helpers that used to create form elements.
b. URL helpers – helpers that creating links.
c. Text helpers – helpers used in various text formatting routines.
d. File helpers – helpers used file related functionalities.
e. Cookie – helpers perform set and read cookies.

18. Differentiate Helper and Library?

Helpers are file contains collection of functions in a particular category. Helpers are written in procedural programming. Every helper performs particular functionality. Helpers can be used in Model, View and Controllers.

Libraries are the classes located in libraries directory. These libraries are located in the system/libraries folder. Libraries are used creating instance of library. Libraries are loaded within a controller using a following function initialization.

$this->load->library ('classname');

19. What are the hooks in Codeigniter?

Hooks is the feature or technique provided in Codeigniter means to change or modify the inner workings of the framework without hacking the core files.

20. What are the different types of hooks in Codeigniter?

There are different types of hooks available in CodeIgniter -

a. Pre_controller_constructor
b. Pre_controller
c. Post_constroller
d. Pre_system
e. Post_system
f. Cache_override
g. Display_override

21. How to enable hooks in Codeigniter?

The hook feature perform enabled globally by setting the following file

Application/config/Config.php file

$config['enablehooks'] = TRUE

22. What is official website of Codeigniter?

http://www.codeigniter.com

23. How to destroy all session in Codeigniter?

Destroy all session in Codeigniter using following method.

$this->session->sess_destroy();

24. What is the process to load multiple helper files?

$this->load->helper (array ('helperfile1', 'helperfile2', 'helperfile3'));

25. How to get random records in MySQL using Codeigniter?

Display random records in MySQL using CodeIgniter

$this->db->order_by ('id','RANDOM');

26. How to print SQL statements in CodeIgniter model.

$this->db->last_query();

27. Write down file name in routes are configure or defined?

Routed is Codeigniter in defined in following file.

Application/config/routes.php file.

28. Explain routing in Codeigniter

Routing is URL access technique in Codeigniter configure URL as per requirement rather than accessing it directly from the browsers. Using routing user having to freedom to customize own URL pattern. After matching URL pattern with requested URL. It will trigger the appropriate controller and function.

29. Explain how you can enable CSRF protection in CodeIgniter?

CSRF protection in CodeIgniter is enabling using following setting in

application/config/config.php file

$config ['csrf_protection'] = TRUE;

30. How do you set default time zone in CodeIgniter?

By implement following function in index.php
date_default_timezone_set('Asia/Kolkata');

31. What is URL structure in Codeigniter?

The basic URL structure in Codeigniter is given below
http://localhost/Users/Userino/param1/param2

a. Server Name – localhost
b. Controller Name – Users
c. Function Name – Userinfo
d. Parameters Name – param1/param2

32. How can Codeigniter prevent from the CSRF?

There are many ways to prevent Codeigniter from CSRF. One of them is add hidden field in each web page which is known as CSRF token. This token is matched with random session value of user. If the values are same then the request is secure. If form helper is implemented in controller then form_open function add csrf hidden field in form.

33. What is inhibitor in CodeIgniter?

An error handler class in CodeIgniter is known as Inhibitor. This class contains PHP like functions set_error_handler, register_shutdown_function and set_exception_handler. The collection of functions manages different types of errors. The errors are categories in exceptions, parse errors and fatal errors.

34. What is get_instance function in CodeIgniter?

Get_instance function is act as global method or function. It returns the instance of controller class in CodeIgniter.

35. Explain Routing in CodeIgniter.

Routing in the CodeIgniter is the technique or way to rewrite a URL as per the user requirement. Routing provides facility to create URL SEO friendly instead of using predefined URL.

CHAPTER THREE

Laravel Interview Questions and Answers

1. What is Laravel Framework?

Laravel is open source Framework.

It is free to use framework.

It is MVC- Model View Controller based architecture framework.

By using Laravel web applications develop quickly and easily.

It is released under MIT License.

2. Who invent or launched Laravel Framework?

Taylor Otwell launched Laravel Framework in year 2011.

3. What is current version of Laravel Framework?

Latest Laravel version is 9, Released on February 2022.

4. List Features of Laravel Framework.

Following are the **features** of the **Laravel** framework.

Blade Template Engine

Website development is more secure and scalable.

Eloquent ORM – Object Relational Mapping.

It supports MVC architecture.

Query Builder

Migrations

Reverse Routing

Database Seeding

Restful Controllers

Unit Testing

Model Classes and Directory

5. What is the database supported by Laravel framework?

The database supported by Laravel Framework.

MySQL

PostgreSQL

SQL Server

SQLite

6. List default packages of Laravel Framework.

Default packages in Laravel Framework. -

Scout

Socialite

Passport

Envoy

Cashier

Horizon

7. What is the different artisan commands used in Laravel Framework?

The different artisan commands are –

a. Php artisan make: model;
b. Php artisan make: controller;
c. Php artisan make: middleware;
d. Php artisan make: model;
e. Php artisan make: migration;
f. Php artisan make: auth;

g. Php artisan make: model;
h. Php artisan up;
a. Php artisan down;
j. Php artisan help;
k. Php artisan list;

8. Does Laravel Framework support Bootstrap Web Design?

Yes, Laravel framework support bootstrap web design.

9. How do we check Laravel current version?

We can check Laravel current version by executing following command–

Php artisan -version

10. How application key generate in Laravel Framework?

To generate application key in Laravel framework -

php artisan key: generate;

11. What is middleware in Laravel?

Middleware in Laravel is the mechanism to filter the http requests. It ensures the authentication of the user to use particular web application. If the user not authenticated, the mechanism will redirect the user to the login page of the web application. The purpose of the middleware is to check the user is authenticated or not for the application.

12. What are the aggregate methods of Query Builder?

Following are the aggregate methods of Query builder.

1. Sum()
2. Avg()
3. Min()
4. Max()
5. Count()

13. What is Route in Laravel?

Laravel routes are available in route file within route directory. The routes are defined in routes/web.php file for web navigation. A route is an endpoint defined by a Uniform Resource Identifier.

14. Explain Reverse Routing in Laravel?

It is a technique or way to generate URL based on name or symbol. It is helpful for Laravel application.

15. How to enable query log in Laravel?

enableQueryLog method to enable query log in Laravel.

16. What is Service Container?

Service container is the tool to provide facility for dependency injection in Laravel.

17. How to register Service Provider?

Service Provider register using app.php configuration file. This is located in config/app.php folder. The configuration file having in which we can register class name.

18. Describe Validation Concepts in Laravel.

In Laravel Validation is done using validatesRequest class. validatesRequest having methods or functions to validate the requests coming from the user. Validation is important in Laravel application before storing data in database. It checks the data is in required format or not.

19. Describe directory structure of Laravel Framework

Directory structure of Laravel Framework is –

1. **App** – This directory contains Models, Providers, Exceptions and Http. Within Http directory controllers, middleware, repository and services are available inside this folder. It is important folder inside it code is present.

2. **Config** – In this folder Laravel applications configuration files present.
3. **Database** – In this folder Factories, Migrations and seeders files are available.
4. **Public** – This folder contains application template file information and assets of application.
5. **Resources** – Resources contains application views.
6. **Routes** –**Web** application and **API** routes files are available in routes folder.

20. Where is Facades located in Laravel?

Facades are located in illuminate/support/facades path in Laravel framework.

21. What is dependency injection?

Dependency injection is mechanism or method. In this mechanism one objet is dependent to other object.

22. List dependency injection types?

There are three types of dependency injection –

1. Setter injection
2. Constructor injection
3. Interface injection

23. Explain PHP artisan.

PHP artisan is 'Command Line Interface' using it we can develop Laravel web application. As per our requirement commands are executed through PHP artisan.

24. Laravel MVC framework.

Laravel framework based on Model, View and Controller pattern -

a. Model – Model classes are use to handle database table and application logic.

b. View – View act as User Interface for Laravel application.
c. Controller – Controller in Laravel act as bridge between Model and View.

25. Explain Composer.

Composer is the tool used as a dependency manager for PHP. It provides facility to manage application level dependencies and libraries for PHP.

26. What is Migration?

Migration is the concept used for the version control for the database system. Migration allows share application and while sharing application it maintains database consistency. We can generate migration using PHP artisan commands.

27. What is a concept contract in Laravel?

Core services are provided by Contracts. Contracts are set of interfaces in Laravel.

28. Types of relationships in Laravel Eloquent.

The types of relationships in Laravel Eloquent –

a. One to One
b. One to Many
c. Many to Many
d. Has Many
e. Polymorphic

29. Explain use of cursor method?

The use of cursor method is to reduce the memory usage and accelerates the performance.

30. Explain dd() function in Laravel.

dd() function is used to use the display content of variable on browser. dd() function long form is Dump and Die.

31. Is Laravel support caching concept?

Yes, Laravel support caching concepts. Redis and Memcachedbackend support it.

32. What is faker in Laravel?

Faker is the functionality to create the fake data. This fake data is used or required for the application testing purpose.

Faker is used to generate different types of data – 1. Address 2. Number 3. DateTime.

33. What is Auth in Laravel?

Auth is the concept used for the user authentication in Laravel. In auth process user can identify by its credentials username and password from database. The credentials are handled with the help of session in Laravel to authenticate user. Auth is the inbuilt-system provided by the Laravel. Auth is implemented using php artisan command – php artisan makc:auth

34. How to remove public from the URL.

The steps to remove public from the URL –

1. Take copy of .htaccess file from the public directory and paste it into root directory of Laravel application.
2. In root directory rename server.php file to index.php file.
3. Refresh the application page.

35. Which function is used to check table is present or not in database?

To check whether thc tablc is present or not in database by using hasTable() function;

36. Differentiate insert() and insertGetId() function in Laravel.

Both insert() and insertGetId() function used to insert a record into table. In case of insert() function there is no need to auto incremented ID. But insertGetId() function is used when the ID field is auto incremented.

37. What is the use of @include.

@include is used to add or include the view file to another view file. By using @include add one or more view template files.

38. What are the inbuilt authentication controllers?

The inbuilt authentication controllers –

1. ForgotPasswordController
2. LoginController
3. RegisterController
4. ResetPasswordController
5. VerificationController

CHAPTER FOUR

MySQL Interview Questions and Answers

1. How to create connection in MySQL database?

By using mysql_connect function as follows create connection to MySQL database.

mysql_connect (servername, username, password);

2. How to escape data storing into the database?

addslashes function is used to before storing the data into the database.

3. How to remove escape characters from the string?

Escape characters are removed from the string by using **stripslashes** function.

4. List different tables present in the MySQL?

Following are the tables present in the MySQL. 5 Types of tables present in the MySQL.

1. InnoDB
2. Merge
3. Heap
4. ISAM

5. MyISAM

5. What are heap tables?

Heap tables are basically user for high speed storage on the temporary basis. They are present in memory.

AUTO_INCREMENT feature isn't supported.

INDEXES should not be NULL in heap tables.

Comparison type of operators allowed in heap tables like =, <,>, =>, <=.

BLOB or TEXT fields are not supported in heap tables.

6. Differentiate between Drop and Truncate Table command.

Drop table command deletes the table and data. While truncate table command delete the data of table not the structure of the table.

7. What is the maximum length of field, table and database name in MySQL?

Maximum length of the field, table and database name is 64 characters.

8. How can get Current Date in MySQL?

Current Date in MySQL print using –

SELECT CURDATE();

SELECT CURRENT_DATE();

9. How can get Current Time in MySQL?

Current Time in MySQL print using –

SELECT CURTIME();

SELECT CURRENT_TIME();

10. How can escape automatically incoming data?

By enabling Magic quotes entry in the configuration file of the PHP escape automatically incoming data.

11. Differentiate between CHAR and VARCHAR Data Types.

Both data type stores character type data. Char stores fixed size character data. VARCHAR stores variable size character data.

12. How can we calculate days from current date in MySQL?

By using DATEDIFF function we can calculate number of days from current date.

SELECT DATEDIFF (NOW (),'2022-01-01');

13. Difference between Order By and Group By Clause in MySQL.

Order by clause is basically used to sort the rows or result set of query either in descending or ascending order. By default order by clause return result in ascending order. Group by clause is return result set in group of rows having same value. Group by clause is used in select statement before the order by keyword.

14. What are the MySQL database Files?

.myd – .myd extension type file stores data.

.frm – .frm extension type file stores table structure.

.myi – .myiextension type file stores index.

15. Which functions used to encrypt and decrypt data in MySQL?

In MySQL AES_ENCRYPT() function used to encrypt data, and AES_DECRYPT() function used to decrypt data.

16. In MySQL way to increase performance of Select query?

Select query is used to fetch records from table. Use LIMIT to fetch specific number of records from result set. Use proper Join like Left or Right Join as per SELECT query requirement from one or two tables instead of Full join.

17. How to repair MySQL Table?

MySQL table repaired by executing following commands

a. Table name is **Student**
b. REPAIR TABLE Student
c. REPAIR TABLE Student Quick

(By using the Quick – Only index tree repaired)

d. REPAIR TABLE Student Extende

(By using the Extended – index will create row by row)

18. What is default port no of MySQL Server?

3306 is the default port number of MySQL Server.

19. Differentiate between FLOAT and DOUBLE?

In FLOAT type floating point numbers are stored with eight place accuracy.

In DOUBLE type Floating point numbers are stored with eighteen place accuracy.

20. What is the command to get current MySQL version?

To get the current MySQL version the command is SELECT VERSION();

21. What are the different types of drivers available in MySQL?

The drivers are available in MySQL.

a. PHP Driver
b. Python Driver
c. Perl Driver
d. JDBC Driver
e. ODBC Driver

22. What is the roll of myisamchk?

Myisamchk compress the tables.

CHAPTER FIVE

Javascript Interview Questions and Answers

1. What is JavaScript?

JavaScript is interpreted scripting language.

It is light weighted, and used for client side validation.

It supports object oriented capabilities.

The core of the language implemented in different types of browsers.

It is developed by Netscape Inc.

2. Who invented JavaScript?

Brendan Eich, developed Javascript in 1995. Initially it is called as Live Script and later it is known as name JavaScript.

3. List Data Types of Javascript.

Two Types of Data Types of Javascript –

1. Primitive Data Types.

Number

String

Boolean

NULL

Undefined

Symbol

2. Non Primitive Data Types.

Array

Object

4. Does Javascript is case sensitive language?

Yes, JavaScript is case sensitive language.

5. What are the ways to create objects in Javascript?

Objects can create in Javascript as –

1. Creating instance of array
2. By array constructor

6. What are pop boxes in JavaScript?

Pop boxes available in JavaScript –

a. Alert Box
b. Confirm Box
c. Prompt Box

7. How to create an object in Javascript?

Javascript object is created using object literal as –

Var student {
Name :"Amar",
Age:18,
Class:12,
Division:"A"
}

8. What are the types of functions in JavaScript?

In Javascript two types of functions are available

1. **Named Functions**
2. **Anonymous functions**

9. What is isNan Function?

isNan function checks the value of argument is number or not. If it is number it returns true otherwise false.

10. What is 'this' keyword in JavaScript?

'this ' keyword is used as it refers the object from where it is called.

11. Differentiate between ViewState and SessionState?

ViewState is related specific to a page in session. SessionState is specific to user's information which is accessed in all subsequent pages of web application.

12. Is Javascript support automatic type conversion?

Yes, Javascript support automatic type conversion.

13. Difference between "==" and "==="?

"==" operator checks only for the equality of the value. "===" is check value of equality of the variable with data type of the variables.

14. What is NULL value in Javascript?

NULL in JavaScript represents no value for variable. Also represents as no object.

15. What is mean by undefined value?

Undefined variable means variable doesn't exist used in the code.

CHAPTER SIX

JQuery Interview Questions and Answers

1. What is JQuery?

JQuery is rich set of JavaScript Library.

It supports different types of browsers.

It is used for event handling, animation, validation purpose.

JQuery is fast and light weight.

JQuery is easy to use and learn.

It is used in Ajax Interactions.

2. Explain JQuery effect methods.

JQuery effect methods provide special effects to HTML elements as per task requirement. JQuery methods are –

Toggle()

fadeIn()

fadeOut()

fadeToggle()

animate()

show()

hide()

3. Is JQuery work for both HTML and XML Document?

No, JQuery only work for HTML document. Not for XML Document.

4. What is the css() method in JQuery?

In JQuery css() method is used to set or get the properties of HTML elements.

5. Which function is starting execution point of JQuery?

$(document).ready() function is starting execution point of JQuery.

6. Is it possible to use multiple document.ready() function on same page?

Yes, it is possible to use multiple document.ready() function on same page.

7. What are the selectors in JQuery?

The function of the selectors is to search or find the HTML elements in JQuery for further process.

8. What are types of electors in JQuery?

Name Selector

#Id Selector

.Class Selector

Attribute Selector

Universal(*) Selector

9. Differentiate ID and Class Selectors in JQuery?

To select only one element ID selector is used. To select more than one or group of elements selection process uses css Class Selectors.

10. What is Ajax?

Ajax means Asynchronous Javascript XML. It is the technique to get or retrieve data from web page or modify content of page without refreshing entire web page.

11. What are the methods used in Ajax?

The methods used in Ajax interaction are – load(), get(), post().

9 798887 725536

Printed by Libri Plureos GmbH in Hamburg,
Germany